Rounded Vowel Finals in Alternate Pronunciation of Mandarin Characters

by

Stephen M Kraemer

In the Chinese writing system, a number of characters have more than one pronunciation in Mandarin. In many cases, these pronunciations are related phonetically, i.e., share one or more of phonetic features. In the current volume, characters whose pronunciations consist of all vowel finals are given. In addition, each character pronunciation contains one rounded vowel. Characters are then arranged according to the phonetic patterns exhibited by their finals in Mandarin.

Character pronunciations that have the same tone (Tone Perfect) are also listed separately along with each final pattern.
Phonetic patterns for character initials or all vowel (V) segments are also given.

Characters are presented that exhibit different finals in their pronunciation. Therefore, character pronunciations that have the same segment (or same consonants and vowels) and differ only in tone, or have the same finals are not included in this study:

Mandarin character pronunciations are given in pinyin. Characters and their pronunciations are taken from Xinhua Zidian (1971).

All Vowel Final Variation with Rounded Vowels

All Back, Rounded Vowel Finals (o[o]/uo[uo]) Tone Perfect

喔 ō, wō

V Segment

o/w

All Back, Rounded Vowel Finals (o[o]/uo[uo])

泺 luò, pō
Voiced Alveolar/Voiceless Bilabial

魄 pò, tuò
魄 tuò, bó
Voiceless Bilabial/ Voiceless Alveolar

All Back Vowel Finals (o[o]/ ao[ɑu])

Tone Perfect

剥 bāo, bō

薄 báo, bó

Voiceless Bilabial Initial Perfect

冒 mào, mò

Voiced Bilabial Initial Perfect

All Back Vowel Finals (o[o]/ ao[ɑu]) 薄 báo, bò Voiceless Bilabial Initial Perfect

All Non-Mid Vowel Finals (o[o]/iao[iɑu]) 朴 pō, piáo 朴 pò, piáo Voiceless Bilabial Initial Perfect

All Back, Rounded Single Vowel Finals (u[u]/o[o]) Tone Perfect

佛 fó, fú

Voiceless Labial Initial Perfect

模 mó, mú

Voiced Bilabial Initial Perfect

All Back, Rounded Single Vowel Finals (u[u]/o[o])

卜 bǔ, bo

朴 pò, pǔ

朴 pǔ, pō

Voiceless Bilabial Initial Perfect

All High, Rounded Single Vowel Finals (u[u]/ü[y]) Tone Perfect

浒 hǔ, xǔ

Velar/Palatal

绿 lǜ, lù

Voiced Alveolar Initial Perfect

畜 xù, chù

Palatal/Voiceless

Retroflex

於 yū, wū

V Segment

y/w

All High, Rounded Single Vowel Finals (u[u]/ü[y])

谷 gǔ, yù

Velar/y

於 yú, wū

V Segment

y/w

俞 yú, shù

y/Voiceless

Retroflex

All Non-Low Vowel Finals (uo[uo]/üe[ye]) High, Rounded Medial Vowel (u[u]/ü[y]) Mid Vowel Rime (o[o]/e[e])

说 shuō, yuè

Voiceless Retroflex/y

All Non-Low Vowel Finals (ui[uei]/üe[ye]) High, Rounded Medial Vowel (u[u]/ü[y]) Mid, Front Vowel (e[e]/e[e]) Tone Perfect 说 shuì, yuè Voiceless Retroflex/y

All Non-Low Vowel Finals
(ui[uei]/ ü[y])
High, Rounded First Vowel
(u[u]/ ü[y])
Tone Perfect
咀 jǔ, zuǐ
Palatal/Dental
蔚 wèi, yù
V Segment
w/y

All Non-Low Vowel Finals
(ui[uei]/ ü[y])
High, Rounded First Vowel
(u[u]/ ü[y])
柜 guì, jǔ
Velar/Palatal
圩 wéi, xū
w/Palatal

All Non-Mid Vowel Finals (uai[uai]/ü[y]) High, Rounded First Vowel (u[u]/ü[y]) Tone Perfect

率 shuài, lǜ

Voiceless Retroflex/Voiced Alveolar

All Vowel Finals (uai[uai]/ ui[uei]) Medial-Ending Perfect (u_i) Tone Perfect Front, Unrounded Rimes (ai[ai]/ ei[ei]) 会 huì, kuài Velar

All Vowel Finals (uai[uai]/ui[uei]) Medial-Ending Perfect (u_i) Front, Unrounded Rimes (ai[ai]/ei[ei])

崴 wǎi, wēi

V Segment

w

All Vowel Finals
(uai[uai]/uo[uo])
Medial Perfect
(u[u])
Tone Perfect
啜 chuò, chuài
Voiceless Retroflex
Initial Perfect

All Vowel Finals
(uai[uai]/uo[uo])
Medial Perfect
(u[u])
掴 guó, guāi
Velar
Initial Perfect

All Non-Low Vowel Finals (u[u]/iu[iou]) High, Back, Rounded Vowel (u[u]/u[u]) Tone Perfect

六 liù, lù
陆 lù, liù
碌 lù, liù
Voiced Alveolar
Initial Perfect
宿 sù, xiù
Dental/Palatal

All Non-Low Vowel Finals (u[u]/iu[iou]) High, Back, Rounded Vowel (u[u]/u[u]) 宿 sù, xiǔ Dental/Palatal

All Back, Rounded Vowel Finals (u[u]/ou[ou])

High, Back, Rounded Vowel (u[u]/u[u])

Tone Perfect

都 dū, dōu

Voiceless Alveolar Initial Perfect

露 lù, lòu
Voiced Alveolar
Initial Perfect
熟 shú, shóu
Voiceless Retroflex
Initial Perfect

All Back, Rounded Vowel Finals (u[u]/ou[ou])

High, Back, Rounded Vowel (u[u]/u[u])

读 dú, dòu

Voiceless Alveolar Initial Perfect

牟 móu, mù

Voiced Bilabial Initial Perfect

All Non-Mid, Back Vowel Finals (u[u]/ao[ɑu]) High, Back, Rounded Vowel (u[u]/o[u]) Tone Perfect

堡 bǎo, bǔ
Voiceless Bilabial
Initial Perfect
暴 bào, pù
瀑 pù, bào
Voiceless Bilabial
姥 mǔ, lǎo
Voiced
Bilabial/Voiced
Alveolar

All Non-Mid, Back Vowel Finals (u[u]/ao[ɑu])

High, Back, Rounded Vowel (u[u]/o[u])

堡 bǎo, pù

Voiceless Bilabial

All Non-Mid, Back
Vowel Finals
(u[u]/ua[uɑ])
High, Back, Rounded
First Vowel
(u[u]/u[u])
Tone Perfect
呱 guā, gū
Velar
Initial Perfect

All Non-Mid, Back
Vowel Finals
(u[u]/ua[uɑ])
High, Back, Rounded
First Vowel
(u[u]/u[u])
呱 gū, guǎ
Velar
Initial Perfect

All Non-Mid Vowel Finals (u[u]/iao[iɑu]) High, Back, Rounded Vowel (u[u]/o[u]) 莩 fú, piǎo Voiceless Labial 朴 pǔ, piáo Voiceless Bilabial Initial Perfect

All Back, Rounded Vowel Finals (u[u]/uo[uo]

High, Back, Rounded Vowel (u[u]/u[u])

Tone Perfect

和 huó, hú

Velar

Initial Perfect

数 shù, shuò
Voiceless Retroflex
Initial Perfect
酢 zuò, cù
Dental

All Back, Rounded Vowel Finals (u[u]/uo[uo] High, Back, Rounded Vowel (u[u]/u[u])

度 dù, duó
Voiceless Alveolar
Initial Perfect
和 huò, hú
Velar
Initial Perfect

数 shǔ, shuò

著 zhù, zhuó

Voiceless Retroflex

Initial Perfect

缩 suō, sù

Dental

Initial Perfect

All Back Vowel Finals (uo[uo]/ao[ɑu])

High, Back, Rounded Vowel (u[u]/o[u])

Tone Perfect

落 luò, lào

络 luò, lào

烙 lào, luò

Voiced Alveolar Initial Perfect

着 zhuó, zháo Voiceless Retroflex Initial Perfect

All Back Vowel Finals (uo[uo]/ao[ɑu]) High, Back, Rounded Vowel (u[u]/o[u])

绰 chuò, chāo

棹 zhào, zhuō

着 zhuó, zhāo

Voiceless Retroflex Initial Perfect

凿 záo, zuò
Dental
Initial Perfect
焯 zhuō, chāo
Voiceless Retroflex

All Back Vowel Finals (uo[uo]/ua[uɑ]) Medial Perfect (u[u]/u[u]) Tone Perfect

挼 ruó, ruá

Voiced Retroflex Initial Perfect

挝 zhuā, wō

Voiceless Retroflex/w

All Back Vowel Finals (uo[uo]/ ua[uɑ]) Medial Perfect (u[u]/ u[u]) 括 kuò, guā Velar

All Non-Mid, Back Vowel Finals (ua[uɑ]/au[ɑu])

High, Back, Rounded Vowel (u[u]/u[u])

Low, Back Vowel (a[ɑ])

Tone Perfect

爪 zhǎo, zhuǎ

Voiceless Retroflex Initial Perfect

All Non-Mid Vowel Finals (ua[uɑ]/uai[uai]) Medial Perfect (u[u]/u[u]) Low Vowel (a[ɑ]/a[a])

划 huà, huai

划 huá, huai

Velar

Initial Perfect

All Non-Mid Vowel Finals (ü[y]/ ua[uɑ]) High Rounded First Vowel (ü[y]/ u[u])

𦍌 xū, huā

Palatal/Velar

All Rounded Vowel Finals (ü[y]/ou[ou]) High Rounded Vowel (ü[y]/u[u]) Tone Perfect

区 qū, ōu

Palatal/o

All Rounded Vowel Finals (ü[y]/ou[ou])

High Rounded Vowel

(ü[y]/u[u])

句 jù, gōu

Palatal/Velar

偻 lǚ, lóu

Voiced Alveolar Initial Perfect

All Rounded Vowel Finals (ü[y]/uo[uo] High Rounded First Vowel (ü[y]/u[u]) 捋 luō, lǚ Voiced Alveolar Initial Perfect

All Vowel Finals (üe[ye]/iao[iɑu]) High, Front Medial Vowel (ü[y]/i[i]) High Rounded Vowel (ü[y]/o[u]) Tone Perfect

嚼 jiáo, jué

削 xiāo, xuē

Palatal

Initial Perfect

疟 nüè, yào

Voiced Alveolar/y

蹻 qiāo, juē

Palatal

约 yuē, yāo
钥 yuè, yào
V Segment
y

All Vowel Finals (üe[ye]/ iao[ou]) High, Front Medial Vowel (ü[y]/i[i]) High Rounded Vowel (ü[y]/o[u])

脚 jiǎo, jué
角 jiǎo, jué
觉 jué, jiào
嚼 jué, jiào
雀 què, qiāo
雀 què, qiǎo
Palatal
Initial Perfect

All Non-Low Vowel Finals (ui[uei]/iu[iou]) High, Back, Rounded Vowel (u[u]/u[u]) High Front, Unrounded Vowel (i[i]/i[i]) Mid Vowel (e[e]/o[o]) Tone Perfect

龟 guī, qiū
Velar/Palatal

All Vowel Finals
(uei[uei]/iau[iɑu])
High, Back, Rounded
Vowel
(u[u]/u[u])
High Front,
Unrounded Vowel
(i[i]/i[i])
尿 niào, suī
Voiced
Alveolar/Dental

All Vowel Finals (iao[iɑu]/iu[iou]) Medial-Ending Perfect (i_u) BackVowel Rimes (ao[ɑu]/ou[ou]) Tone Perfect

缪 miào, miù
Voiced Bilabial
Initial Perfect
繇 yóu, yáo
V Segment
y

All Vowel Finals
(iao[iɑu]/iu[iou])
Medial-Ending
Perfect
(i_u)
BackVowel Rimes
(ao[ɑu]/ou[ou])
湫 qiū, jiǎo
Palatal

All Non-Mid Vowel Finals (iao[iɑu]/ ao[ɑu]) Rime Perfect (ao[ɑu]) Tone Perfect

潦 lǎo, liǎo

Voiced Alveolar Initial Perfect

缲 qiāo, sāo
Palatal/Dental
陶 táo, yáo
Voiceless Alveolar/y
苕 tiáo, sháo
Voiceless
Alveolar/Voiceless
Retroflex

All Non-Mid Vowel Finals (iao[iɑu]/ao[ɑu]) Rime Perfect (ao[ɑu])

剿 jiǎo, chāo

鞘 qiào, shāo

Voiceless Retroflex/Palatal

All Non-Low Vowel Finals (iu[iou]/ou[ou]) Rime Perfect (ou[ou]) Tone Perfect

仇 chóu, qiú

臭 chòu, xiù

Voiceless

Retroflex/Palatal

All Non-Low Vowel Finals (iu[iou]/ou[ou]) Rime Perfect (ou[ou])

缪 móu, miù

Voiced Bilabial Initial Perfect

All Vowel Finals

(iao[iɑu]/ uo[uo])

High, Medial Vowel

(i[i]/ u[u]

High, Back, Rounded Vowel

(u[u]/ u[u])

Back Vowel Rimes

(ao[ɑu]/ o[o])

缴 jiǎo, zhuó

Palatal/ Voiceless Retroflex

All Vowel Finals (iao[iɑu]/ou[ou]) Ending Perfect (u) BackVowel Rimes (ao[ɑu]/ou[ou]) 缪 miào, móu Voiced Bilabial Initial Perfect

All Back Vowel Finals (ao[ɑu]/ou[ou]) Ending Perfect (u)

Tone Perfect

啁 zhōu, zhāo

Voiceless Retroflex Initial Perfect

All Vowel Finals (ao[ɑu]/iu[iou]) Ending Perfect (u) BackVowel Rimes (ao[ɑu]/ou[ou]) Tone Perfect 拗 ào, niù a/Voiced Alveolar

All Vowel Finals (ao[ɑu]/iu[iou]) Ending Perfect (u) BackVowel Rimes (ao[ɑu]/ou[ou]) 拗 ǎo, niù a/Voiced Alveolar

References

Cheng, C.C. (1973). *A synchronic phonology of Mandarin Chinese*. The Hague: Mouton.

DeFrancis, John. (1970). *Index volume*. New Haven: Yale University Press.

Handian [<汉典>, '字典']. Online Chinese dictionary. (2004 – 2015). http://www.zdic.net

Kratochvil, Paul. (1968). *The Chinese language today: Features of an emerging standard*. London: Hutchinson & Co., Ltd.

Xinhua zidian (New China dictionary). (1971). Beijing: Shangwu Yinshuguan. [<新华字典>, 1971, 北京: 商务印书馆.]

Zhou, Youguang. (1980). *Hanzi shengpang duyin biancha* (A handy look up for the pronunciation of phonetics in Chinese characters). Jilin: Jilin Remnin Chubanshe.
[周 有光, 1980, <汉字声旁读音便查>，吉林：吉林人民出版社.]

Books on the Chinese Writing System by Stephen M. Kraemer

Available on Amazon.com

(www.amazon.com/author/stephenkraemer)

Kraemer, Stephen M. (2017a). *Let's Learn Mandarin Phonics. Seven Basic Phonetic Patterns of Commonly Occurring Chinese Characters.* CreateSpace Independent Publishing Platform.

Kraemer, Stephen M. (2017b). *Let's Learn Mandarin Phonics-2. Final and Final-Tone Perfect Phonetic Patterns of Common Chinese Characters.* CreateSpace Independent Publishing Platform.

Kraemer, Stephen M. (2018a). *Let's Learn Mandarin Phonics-3. Rime Clue, Rime-Tone Clue, Ending Clue, Ending-Tone Clue Phonetic Patterns of Common Chinese Characters.* CreateSpace Independent Publishing Platform.

Kraemer, Stephen M. (2018b). *Let's Learn Mandarin Phonics-4. Initial Clue, Initial-Tone Clue, Tone-Clue and Related Phonetic Patterns of Common Chinese Characters.* CreateSpace Independent Publishing Platform.

Kraemer, Stephen M. (2018c). *Let's Learn Mandarin Phonics-5. Vowel Phonetic Clues for Common Chinese Characters.* CreateSpace Independent Publishing Platform.

Kraemer, Stephen M. (2018d). *Phonetic Clues for Learning Common Chinese Characters.* CreateSpace Independent Publishing Platform.

Kraemer, Stephen M. (2018e). *A Phonetic Guide to Learning Chinese Characters.* CreateSpace Independent Publishing Platform.

Kraemer, Stephen M. (2018f). *Let*'s *Learn Pinyin Final "i" Chinese Characters in Mandarin*. CreateSpace Independent Publishing Platform.

Kraemer, Stephen M. (2018g). *Homorganic Initial Patterns in Common Mandarin Chinese Characters.* CreateSpace Independent Publishing Platform.

Kraemer, Stephen M. (2018h). *Let*'s *Learn Pinyin Final "u/ü" Patterns in Mandarin Chinese Characters*. CreateSpace Independent Publishing Platform.

Kraemer, Stephen M. (2018i). *Coronal Initial Patterns in Common Mandarin Chinese Characters*. CreateSpace Independent Publishing Platform.

Kraemer, Stephen M. (2018j). *Voiceless Alveolar/Retroflex Initial Patterns in Mandarin Chinese Characters*. CreateSpace Independent Publishing Platform.

Kraemer, Stephen M. (2018k). *Velar/Palatal Initial Patterns in Mandarin Chinese Characters*. CreateSpace Independent Publishing Platform.

Kraemer, Stephen M. (2018l). *Pinyin 'an' Rime Patterns in Mandarin Chinese Characters*. CreateSpace Independent Publishing Platform.

Kraemer, Stephen M. (2018m). *Let's Learn Pinyin "n/ng" Ending Patterns in Mandarin Chinese Characters*. CreateSpace Independent Publishing Platform.

Kraemer, Stephen M. (2018n). *Final Patterns in Pinyin "ng" Ending Mandarin Chinese Characters*. CreateSpace Independent Publishing Platform.

Kraemer, Stephen M. (2019). *Initial Perfect and Initial-Tone Perfect Patterns in Mandarin Chinese Characters*. Independent Publishing Platform.

Kraemer, Stephen M. (2019a). *Initial-Rime Perfect and Initial-Ending Perfect Patterns in Mandarin Chinese Characters*. Independent Publishing Platform.

Kraemer, Stephen M. (2019b). *Similar Vowel Patterns in Initial-Perfect Mandarin Chinese Characters.* Independent Publishing Platform.

Kraemer, Stephen M. (2019c). *Homorganic Variation in the Pronunciation of Chinese Characters in Mandarin.* Independent Publishing Platform.

Kraemer, Stephen M. (2019d). *Coronal Variation in the Pronunciation of Chinese Characters in Mandarin.* Independent Publishing Platform.

Kraemer, Stephen M. (2019e). *Pronunciation Variation in V and VC1 Segment Characters in Mandarin.* Independent Publishing Platform.

Kraemer, Stephen M. (2019f). *Dorsal/Coronal Variation in the Pronunciation of Chinese Characters in Mandarin*. Independent Publishing Platform.

Kraemer, Stephen M. (2019g). *A Phonetic Guide to Mandarin Chinese Characters in Color*. Independent Publishing Platform.

Kraemer, Stephen M. (2019h). *Phonetic Clues for Mandarin Chinese Characters in Color*. Independent Publishing Platform.

Kraemer, Stephen M. (2019i). *More Phonetic Clues for Mandarin Chinese Characters in Color*. Independent Publishing Platform.

Kraemer, Stephen M. (2019j). *Even More Phonetic Clues for Mandarin Chinese Characters in Color*. Independent Publishing Platform.

Kraemer, Stephen M. (2019k). *Phonetic Patterns in Mandarin Chinese Characters*. Independent Publishing Platform.

Kraemer, Stephen M. (2019l). *More Phonetic Patterns in Mandarin Chinese Characters*. Independent Publishing Platform.

Kraemer, Stephen M. (2019m). *Even More Phonetic Patterns in Mandarin Chinese Characters*. Independent Publishing Platform.

Kraemer, Stephen M. (2019n). *Still More Phonetic Clues for Mandarin Chinese Characters in Color*. Independent Publishing Platform.

Kraemer, Stephen M. (2019o). *More and More Phonetic Clues for Mandarin Chinese Characters in Color*. Independent Publishing Platform.

Kraemer, Stephen M. (2019p). *Still More Phonetic Patterns in Mandarin Chinese Characters.* Independent Publishing Platform.

Kraemer, Stephen M. (2019q). *A Phonetic Color Guide to Mandarin Chinese Characters*. Independent Publishing Platform.

Kraemer, Stephen M. (2019r). *Pinyin "ch/c" Initial Patterns in Mandarin Chinese Characters*. Independent Publishing Platform.

Kraemer, Stephen M. (2019s). *Pinyin "zh/z" Initial Patterns in Mandarin Chinese Characters*. Independent Publishing Platform.

Kraemer, Stephen M. (2019t). *Pinyin "sh/s" Initial Patterns in Mandarin Chinese Characters*. Independent Publishing Platform.

Kraemer, Stephen M. (2019u). *Pinyin "sh/x" Initial Patterns in Mandarin Chinese Characters*. Independent Publishing Platform.

Kraemer, Stephen M. (2019v). *Pinyin "zh/j" Initial Patterns in Mandarin Chinese Characters*. Independent Publishing Platform.

Kraemer, Stephen M. (2019w). *Pinyin "z/c" Initial Patterns in Mandarin Chinese Characters*. Independent Publishing Platform.

Kraemer, Stephen M. (2019x). *Dental Initial Patterns in Mandarin Chinese Characters*. Independent Publishing Platform.

Kraemer, Stephen M. (2019y). *Dental/Palatal Initial Patterns in Mandarin Chinese Characters*. Independent Publishing Platform.

Kraemer, Stephen M. (2019z). *Retroflex/Palatal Initial Patterns in Mandarin Chinese Characters*. Independent Publishing Platform.

Kraemer, Stephen M. (2019aa). *Final Patterns in Velar/Palatal Mandarin Chinese Characters*. Independent Publishing Platform.

Kraemer, Stephen M. (2019ab). *Pinyin "e/i" Single Vowel Patterns in Mandarin Chinese Characters*. Independent Publishing Platform.

Kraemer, Stephen M. (2019ac). *Pinyin "a/e" Single Vowel Patterns in Mandarin Chinese Characters*. Independent Publishing Platform.

Kraemer, Stephen M. (2019ad). *Retroflex/Dental Initial Patterns in Mandarin Chinese Characters*. Independent Publishing Platform.

Kraemer, Stephen M. (2019ae). *Pinyin "ch/sh" Initial Patterns in Mandarin Chinese Characters*. Independent Publishing Platform.

Kraemer, Stephen M. (2019af). *Pinyin "zh/sh" Initial Patterns in Mandarin Chinese Characters*. Independent Publishing Platform.

Kraemer, Stephen M. (2019ag). *Pinyin "zh/ch" Initial Patterns in Mandarin Chinese Characters*. Independent Publishing Platform.

Kraemer, Stephen M. (2019ah). *Retroflex Initial Patterns in Mandarin Chinese Characters*. Independent Publishing Platform.

Kraemer, Stephen M. (2019ai). *Palatal/ "l" Initial Patterns in Mandarin Chinese Characters*. Independent Publishing Platform.

Kraemer, Stephen M. (2019aj). *Alveolar/Palatal Initial Patterns in Mandarin Chinese Characters*. Independent Publishing Platform.

Kraemer, Stephen M. (2019ak). *Retroflex/Voiced Alveolar Initial Patterns in Mandarin Chinese Characters*. Independent Publishing Platform.

Kraemer, Stephen M. (2019al). *Pinyin "y" Patterns in Mandarin Chinese Characters*. Independent Publishing Platform.

Kraemer, Stephen M. (2019am). *Pinyin "w" and "w/y" Patterns in Mandarin Chinese Characters*. Independent Publishing Platform.

Kraemer, Stephen M. (2019an). *V Segment Patterns in Mandarin Chinese Characters*. Independent Publishing Platform.

Kraemer, Stephen M. (2019ao). *Pinyin "ai/i" Vowel Patterns in Mandarin Chinese Characters*. Independent Publishing Platform.

Kraemer, Stephen M. (2019ap). *Phonetic Patterns in Mandarin Chinese Characters: Pinyin "a" Finals and Unrounded Diphthongs*. Independent Publishing Platform.

Kraemer, Stephen M. (2019aq). *Phonetic Patterns in Mandarin Chinese Characters: Pinyin "e" Finals and Unrounded Diphthongs*. Independent Publishing Platform.

Kraemer, Stephen M. (2019ar). *Phonetic Patterns in Mandarin Chinese Characters: Unrounded Diphthong Finals*. Independent Publishing Platform.

Kraemer, Stephen M. (2019as). *Phonetic Patterns in Mandarin Chinese Characters: Rounded Medial Vowels in V Finals*. Independent Publishing Platform.

Kraemer, Stephen M. (2019at). *Phonetic Patterns in Mandarin Chinese Characters: Rounded Medial and Rounded Ending Vowels in V Finals*. Independent Publishing Platform.

Kraemer, Stephen M. (2019au). *Phonetic Patterns in Mandarin Chinese Characters: Pinyin "u" and Rounded Medial Vowels in V Finals*. Independent Publishing Platform.

Kraemer, Stephen M. (2019av). *Phonetic Patterns of Chinese Characters: Velar / "w" and Velar / "y" in Mandarin*. Independent Publishing Platform.

Kraemer, Stephen M. (2019aw). *Phonetic Patterns of Chinese Characters: Alveolar / "y" in Mandarin*. Independent Publishing Platform.

Kraemer, Stephen M. (2019ax). *Phonetic Patterns of Chinese Characters: Retroflex / "y" in Mandarin*. Independent Publishing Platform.

Kraemer, Stephen M. (2019ay). *Phonetic Patterns of Chinese Characters: Palatal / "y" in Mandarin*. Independent Publishing Platform.

Kraemer, Stephen M. (2019az). *Phonetic Patterns of Chinese Characters: Pinyin "g/k" in Mandarin*. Independent Publishing Platform.

Kraemer, Stephen M. (2019aaa). *Phonetic Patterns of Chinese Characters: Pinyin "g/h" in Mandarin*. Independent Publishing Platform.

Kraemer, Stephen M. (2019aab). *Phonetic Patterns of Chinese Characters: Pinyin "h/k" in Mandarin*. Independent Publishing Platform.

Kraemer, Stephen M. (2019aac). *Phonetic Patterns of Chinese Characters: Velar Initials in Mandarin*. Independent Publishing Platform.

Kraemer, Stephen M. (2019aad). *Phonetic Patterns in Mandarin Chinese Characters: Pinyin "i/ie" Finals*. Independent Publishing Platform.

Kraemer, Stephen M. (2019aae). *Phonetic Patterns in Mandarin Chinese Characters: Pinyin "i/a" and "i/ei" Finals*. Independent Publishing Platform.

Kraemer, Stephen M. (2019aaf). *Phonetic Patterns of Chinese Characters: Pinyin "d/t" Initials in Mandarin*. Independent Publishing Platform.

Kraemer, Stephen M. (2019aag). *Phonetic Patterns of Chinese Characters: Alveolar Initials in Mandarin*. Independent Publishing Platform.

Kraemer, Stephen M. (2019aah). *Phonetic Patterns of Chinese Characters: Pinyin "b/p" Initials in Mandarin*. Independent Publishing Platform.

Kraemer, Stephen M. (2019aai). *Phonetic Patterns of Chinese Characters: Pinyin "f/b" and "f/p" Initials in Mandarin*. Independent Publishing Platform.

Kraemer, Stephen M. (2019aaj). *Phonetic Patterns of Chinese Characters: Labial Initials in Mandarin*. Independent Publishing Platform.

Kraemer, Stephen M. (2019aak). *Phonetic Patterns in Mandarin Chinese Characters: Pinyin "uo" and Unrounded V Finals*. Independent Publishing Platform.

Kraemer, Stephen M. (2019aal). *Phonetic Patterns in Mandarin Chinese Characters: Pinyin "u" and Unrounded V Finals*. Independent Publishing Platform.

Kraemer, Stephen M.(2019aam). *Phonetic Patterns in Mandarin Chinese Characters: Pinyin "u" and Rounded Ending Vowels in V Finals*. Independent Publishing Platform.

Kraemer, Stephen M.(2019aan). *Phonetic Patterns in Mandarin Chinese Characters: Rounded Ending Vowels in V Finals*. Independent Publishing Platform.

Kraemer, Stephen M.(2019aao). *Phonetic Patterns in Mandarin Chinese Characters: Pinyin "an"/ "en"/ "in" Finals*. Independent Publishing Platform.

Kraemer, Stephen M.(2019aap). *Phonetic Patterns in Mandarin Chinese Characters: V/VC1 Finals with a Rounded Vowel*. Independent Publishing Platform.

Kraemer, Stephen M.(2019aaq). *Phonetic Patterns in Mandarin Chinese Characters: V Finals with a Rounded Vowel Plus VC1 Finals with Unrounded V*. Independent Publishing Platform.

Kraemer, Stephen M.(2019aar). *Phonetic Patterns in Mandarin Chinese Characters: V/VC1 Finals with Unrounded Vowels*. Independent Publishing Platform.

Kraemer, Stephen M.(2019aas). *Phonetic Patterns in Mandarin Chinese Characters: Pinyin "n" Ending Finals with One Rounded Vowel*. Independent Publishing Platform.

Kraemer, Stephen M.(2019aat). *Phonetic Patterns in Mandarin Chinese Characters: VC1 Finals with One Rounded Vowel*. Independent Publishing Platform.

Kraemer, Stephen M.(2019aau). *Phonetic Patterns in Mandarin Chinese Characters: Pinyin "n" Ending Finals with Rounded and Unrounded Vowels.* Independent Publishing Platform.

Kraemer, Stephen M.(2019aav). *Phonetic Patterns in Mandarin Chinese Characters: VC1 Finals with Rounded and Unrounded Vowels*. Independent Publishing Platform.

Kraemer, Stephen M.(2020). *Phonetic Patterns in Mandarin Chinese Characters: Pinyin "ng" Ending Finals with Unrounded Vowels*. Independent Publishing Platform.

Kraemer, Stephen M.(2020a). *Phonetic Patterns in Mandarin Chinese Characters: Pinyin "n/ng" Ending Finals with Unrounded Vowels*. Independent Publishing Platform.

Kraemer, Stephen M.(2020b). *Phonetic Patterns in Mandarin Chinese Characters: V/VC1 Finals*. Independent Publishing Platform.

Kraemer, Stephen M.(2020c). *Phonetic Patterns in Mandarin Chinese Characters: VC1 Finals with Unrounded Vowels*. Independent Publishing Platform.

Kraemer, Stephen M.(2020d). *Phonetic Patterns in Mandarin Chinese Characters: V Finals with a Rounded Medial Vowel Plus Unrounded V*. Independent Publishing Platform.

Kraemer, Stephen M.(2020e). *Phonetic Patterns in Mandarin Chinese Characters: V Finals with a Rounded Ending Vowel Plus Unrounded V*. Independent Publishing Platform.

Kraemer, Stephen M.(2020f). *Phonetic Patterns in Mandarin Chinese Characters: Labial/Velar Initials and Pinyin "m"/ "w"*. Independent Publishing Platform.

Kraemer, Stephen M.(2020g). *Phonetic Patterns in Mandarin Chinese Characters: Velar/Retroflex Initials*. Independent Publishing Platform.

Kraemer, Stephen M.(2020h). *Phonetic Patterns in Mandarin Chinese Characters: Velar/Alveolar Initials*. Independent Publishing Platform.

Kraemer, Stephen M.(2020i). *Phonetic Patterns in Mandarin Chinese Characters: Palatal Initials*. Independent Publishing Platform.

Kraemer, Stephen M.(2020j). *Phonetic Patterns in Chinese Characters: Pinyin "a/e" Variation in Mandarin*. Independent Publishing Platform.

Kraemer, Stephen M.(2020k). *Phonetic Groups in Chinese Characters: All Unrounded Vowel Finals in Mandarin*. Independent Publishing Platform.

Kraemer, Stephen M.(2020l). *Phonetic Groups in Chinese Characters: All Unrounded Vowel Finals in Mandarin Volume 2*. Independent Publishing Platform.

Kraemer, Stephen M.(2020m). *Phonetic Groups in Chinese Characters: All Unrounded Vowel Finals in Mandarin Volume 3*. Independent Publishing Platform.

Kraemer, Stephen M.(2020n). *Phonetic Groups in Chinese Characters: All Vowel Finals in Mandarin*. Independent Publishing Platform.

Kraemer, Stephen M.(2020o). *Phonetic Groups in Chinese Characters: All Vowel Finals in Mandarin Volume 2*. Independent Publishing Platform.

Kraemer, Stephen M.(2020p). *Phonetic Groups in Chinese Characters: All Vowel Finals in Mandarin Volume 3*. Independent Publishing Platform.

Kraemer, Stephen M.(2020q). *Phonetic Patterns in Mandarin Chinese Characters: Final Perfect with Palatal j/x, q/x Initials*. Independent Publishing Platform.

Kraemer, Stephen M.(2020r). *Phonetic Groups in Chinese Characters: All Unrounded Vowel Finals in Mandarin Volume 4*. Independent Publishing Platform.

Kraemer, Stephen M.(2020s). *Phonetic Groups in Chinese Characters: All Vowel Finals in Mandarin Volume 4*. Independent Publishing Platform.

Kraemer, Stephen M.(2020t). *Phonetic Patterns in Mandarin Chinese Characters: Final Perfect with Palatal j/q Initials*. Independent Publishing Platform.

Kraemer, Stephen M.(2020u). *Phonetic Patterns in Mandarin Chinese Characters: Final Perfect with Palatal Initials*. Independent Publishing Platform.

Kraemer, Stephen M.(2020v). *Phonetic Components for Meaning in Mandarin Chinese Characters*. Independent Publishing Platform.

Kraemer, Stephen M.(2020w). *Phonetic Components for Meaning in Mandarin Chinese Characters Volume 2.* Independent Publishing Platform.

Kraemer, Stephen M.(2020x). *Phonetic Components for Meaning in Mandarin Chinese Characters Volume 3.* Independent Publishing Platform.

Kraemer, Stephen M.(2020y). *Phonetic Components for Meaning in Mandarin Chinese Characters Volume 4.* Independent Publishing Platform.

Kraemer, Stephen M.(2020z). *Phonetic Components for Meaning in Mandarin Chinese Characters Volume 5.* Independent Publishing Platform.

Kraemer, Stephen M.(2020aa). *Phonetic Components for Meaning in Mandarin Chinese Characters Volume 6*. Independent Publishing Platform.

Kraemer, Stephen M.(2020ab). *Phonetic Components for Meaning in Mandarin Chinese Characters Volume 7*. Independent Publishing Platform.

Kraemer, Stephen M.(2020ac). *Semantic Compounds in Mandarin Chinese Characters*. Independent Publishing Platform.

Kraemer, Stephen M.(2020ad). *Patterns and Formulas for Phonetic Groups in Mandarin Chinese Characters*. Independent Publishing Platform.

Kraemer, Stephen M.
(2020ae-ah).
Patterns and Formulas for Phonetic Groups in Mandarin Chinese Characters Volume 2-5. Independent Publishing Platform.

Kraemer, Stephen M.
(2020ai-al).
Patterns and Formulas for Phonetic Groups in Mandarin Chinese Characters Volume 6-9. Independent Publishing Platform.

Kraemer, Stephen M.
(2020am-ap).
Patterns and Formulas for Phonetic Groups in Mandarin Chinese Characters Volume 10-12, 14. Independent Publishing Platform.

Kraemer, Stephen M.
(2020aq-at).
Patterns and Formulas for Phonetic Groups in Mandarin Chinese Characters Volume 15-18.
Independent Publishing Platform.

Kraemer, Stephen M.
(2020au-ax).
Patterns and Formulas for Phonetic Groups in Mandarin Chinese Characters Volume 19-22.
Independent Publishing Platform.

Kraemer, Stephen M.
(2020ay-aab).
Patterns and Formulas for Phonetic Groups in Mandarin Chinese Characters Volume 23-26.
Independent Publishing Platform.

Kraemer, Stephen M.
(2020aac-aaf).
Patterns and Formulas for Phonetic Groups in Mandarin Chinese Characters Volume 27-30.
Independent Publishing Platform.

Kraemer, Stephen M.
(2020aag-aaj).
Patterns and Formulas for Phonetic Groups in Mandarin Chinese Characters Volume 31-34.
Independent Publishing Platform.

Kraemer, Stephen M.
(2020aak-aan).
Patterns and Formulas for Phonetic Groups in Mandarin Chinese Characters Volume 35-38.
Independent Publishing Platform.

Kraemer, Stephen M.
(2020aao-aar).
Patterns and Formulas for Phonetic Groups in Mandarin Chinese Characters Volume 39-42.
Independent Publishing Platform.

Kraemer, Stephen M.
(2020aas-aav).
Patterns and Formulas for Phonetic Groups in Mandarin Chinese Characters Volume 43-46.
Independent Publishing Platform.

Kraemer, Stephen M.
(2020aaw-aaz).
Patterns and Formulas for Phonetic Groups in Mandarin Chinese Characters Volume 47-50.
Independent Publishing Platform.

Kraemer, Stephen M.
(2020aaaa-aaad).
Patterns and Formulas for Phonetic Groups in Mandarin Chinese Characters Volume 51-54.
Independent Publishing Platform.

Kraemer, Stephen M.
(2020aaae-aaah).
Patterns and Formulas for Phonetic Groups in Mandarin Chinese Characters Volume 55-58.
Independent Publishing Platform

Kraemer, Stephen M.(2021).
Patterns and Formulas for Phonetic Groups in Mandarin Chinese Characters Volume 58.
Independent Publishing Platform.

Kraemer, Stephen M.(2021a-d). *Patterns and Formulas for Phonetic Groups in Mandarin Chinese Characters Volume 59-62.* Independent Publishing Platform.

Kraemer, Stephen M.(2021e-f). *Patterns and Formulas for Phonetic Groups in Mandarin Chinese Characters Volume 63-64.* Independent Publishing Platform.

Kraemer, Stephen M.(2021g). *Homographic Components in Homophonous Mandarin Characters*. Independent Publishing Platform.

Kraemer, Stephen M.(2021h). *Homographic Components in Homophonous Mandarin Characters Volume 2*. Independent Publishing Platform.

Kraemer, Stephen M.(2021i). *Homophonous Characters with Two Components in Mandarin*. Independent Publishing Platform.

Kraemer, Stephen M.(2021j). *Homophonous Characters with Two Homographic Components in Mandarin*. Independent Publishing Platform.

Kraemer, Stephen M.(2021k). *Homophonous Characters with Two Components in Mandarin Volume 2*. Independent Publishing Platform.

Kraemer, Stephen M.(2021l). *Phonetic Patterns in Homophonous Mandarin Characters*. Independent Publishing Platform.

Kraemer, Stephen M.(2021m-p). *Phonetic Patterns in Homophonous Mandarin Characters Volume 2-5*. Independent Publishing Platform.

Kraemer, Stephen M.(2021q). *Phonetic Patterns in Homophonous Mandarin Characters Volume 6*. Independent Publishing Platform.

Kraemer, Stephen M.(2021r). *Phonetic Patterns in Homophonous Mandarin Characters Volume 7*. Independent Publishing Platform.

Kraemer, Stephen M.(2021s). *Phonetic Patterns in Homophonous Mandarin Characters Volume 8*. Independent Publishing Platform.

Kraemer, Stephen M.(2021t). *Phonetic Patterns in Homophonous Mandarin Characters Volume 9*. Independent Publishing Platform.

Kraemer, Stephen M.(2021u). *Phonetic Patterns in Homophonous Mandarin Characters Volume 10*. Independent Publishing Platform.

Kraemer, Stephen M.(2021v). *Phonetic Patterns in Homophonous Mandarin Characters Volume 10*. Independent Publishing Platform.

Kraemer, Stephen M.(2021w). *Phonetic Patterns in Homophonous Mandarin Characters Volume 11*. Independent Publishing Platform.

Kraemer, Stephen M.(2021x). *Phonetic Patterns in Homophonous Mandarin Characters Volume 12.* Independent Publishing Platform.

Kraemer, Stephen M.(2021y). *Phonetic Properties of Common Chinese Characters in Mandarin.* Independent Publishing Platform.

Kraemer, Stephen M.(2021z). *Phonetic Properties of Common Chinese Characters in Mandarin Volume 2.* Independent Publishing Platform.

Kraemer, Stephen M.(2021aa). *Phonetic Properties of Common Chinese Characters in Mandarin Volume 3.* Independent Publishing Platform.

Kraemer, Stephen M.(2021ab). *Learn Chinese Characters through Sound and Meaning*. Independent Publishing Platform.

Kraemer, Stephen M.(2021ac). *Learn Chinese Characters through Sound and Meaning Volume 2*. Independent Publishing Platform.

Kraemer, Stephen M.(2021ad). *Learn Chinese Characters through Sound and Meaning Volume 3*. Independent Publishing Platform.

Kraemer, Stephen M.(2021ae). *Learn Chinese Characters through Sound and Meaning Volume 4*. Independent Publishing Platform.

Kraemer, Stephen M.(2021af). *Learn Chinese Characters through Sound and Meaning Volume 5.* Independent Publishing Platform.

Kraemer, Stephen M.(2021ag). *Common Phonetic Chinese Characters in Color.* Independent Publishing Platform.

Kraemer, Stephen M.(2021ah). *Common Phonetic Chinese Characters Traditional and Simplified.* Independent Publishing Platform.

Kraemer, Stephen M.(2021ai). *Phonetic Chinese Characters Traditional and Simplified.* Independent Publishing Platform.

Kraemer, Stephen M.(2021aj). *Phonetic Chinese Characters Traditional and Simplified Volume 2*. Independent Publishing Platform.

Kraemer, Stephen M.(2021ak). *Phonetic Regularity in Traditional Versus Simplified Chinese Characters*. Independent Publishing Platform.

Kraemer, Stephen M.(2021al). *Phonetic Regularity in Traditional Versus Simplified Chinese Characters Volume 2*. Independent Publishing Platform.

Kraemer, Stephen M.(2021am). *Phonetic Regularity in Traditional Versus Simplified Chinese Characters Volume 3*. Independent Publishing Platform.

Kraemer, Stephen M.(2021an). *Phonetic Regularity in Traditional Versus Simplified Chinese Characters Volume 4.* Independent Publishing Platform.

Kraemer, Stephen M.(2021ao). *Phonetic Regularity in Traditional Versus Simplified Chinese Characters Volume 5.* Independent Publishing Platform.

Kraemer, Stephen M.(2021ap). *Phonetic Regularity in Traditional Versus Simplified Chinese Characters Volume 6.* Independent Publishing Platform.

Kraemer, Stephen M.(2021aq). *Phonetic Regularity in Traditional Versus Simplified Chinese Characters Volume 7.* Independent Publishing Platform.

Kraemer, Stephen M.(2021ar). *Phonetic Regularity in Traditional Versus Simplified Chinese Characters Volume 8.* Independent Publishing Platform.

Kraemer, Stephen M.(2021as). *Phonetic Regularity in Traditional Versus Simplified Chinese Characters Volume 9.* Independent Publishing Platform.

Kraemer, Stephen M.(2022). *Phonetic Regularity in Traditional Versus Simplified Chinese Characters Volume 10.* Independent Publishing Platform.

Kraemer, Stephen M.(2022a). *Phonetic Regularity of Similar Form Characters in Mandarin.* Independent Publishing Platform.

Kraemer, Stephen M.(2022b). *Phonetic Regularity of Similar Form Characters in Mandarin Volume 2.* Independent Publishing Platform.

Kraemer, Stephen M.(2022c). *Phonetic Regularity of Homophonous Phonetics in Chinese Writing*. Independent Publishing Platform.

Kraemer, Stephen M.(2022d). *Phonetic Regularity of Homophonous Phonetics in Chinese Writing Volume 2.* Independent Publishing Platform.

Kraemer, Stephen M.(2022e). *Phonetic Regularity of Homophonous Phonetics in Chinese Writing Volume 3.* Independent Publishing Platform.

Kraemer, Stephen M.(2022f). *Phonetic Regularity of Same Segment Phonetics in Chinese Writing.* Independent Publishing Platform.

Kraemer, Stephen M.(2022g). *Phonetic Regularity of Same Segment Phonetics in Chinese Writing Volume 2.* Independent Publishing Platform.

Kraemer, Stephen M.(2022h). *Phonetic Patterns of "Shi" Phonetics in Chinese Writing.* Independent Publishing Platform.

Kraemer, Stephen M.(2022i). *Palatal "i" Phonetics in Chinese Writing.* Independent Publishing Platform.

Kraemer, Stephen M.(2022j). *Dental "i" Phonetics in Chinese Writing.* Independent Publishing Platform.

Kraemer, Stephen M.(2022k).
Alveolar "i" Phonetics in Chinese Writing.
Independent Publishing Platform.

Kraemer, Stephen M.(2022l).
Coronal "e" Phonetics in Chinese Writing.
Independent Publishing Platform.

Kraemer, Stephen M.(2022m).
Coronal "ai" Phonetics in Chinese Writing.
Independent Publishing Platform.

Kraemer, Stephen M.(2022n).
Retroflex "i" Phonetics in Chinese Writing.
Independent Publishing Platform.

Kraemer, Stephen M.(2022o).
Coronal "a" Phonetics in Chinese Writing.
Independent Publishing Platform.

Kraemer, Stephen M.(2022p).
Final "ie" Phonetics in Chinese Writing.
Independent Publishing Platform.

Kraemer, Stephen M.(2022q). *"Yi" Phonetics in Chinese Writing.* Independent Publishing Platform.

Kraemer, Stephen M.(2022r). *A Phonetic Guide to Learning Chinese Characters Volume* 2. Independent Publishing Platform.

Kraemer, Stephen M.(2022s). *Coronal "i" Phonetic Characters in Mandarin Chinese.* Independent Publishing Platform.

Kraemer, Stephen M.(2022t). *Pronunciation Variation in Final "i" Mandarin Chinese Characters.* Independent Publishing Platform.

Kraemer, Stephen M.(2022u). *Unrounded Vowel Finals in Alternate Pronunciation of Mandarin Characters.* Independent Publishing Platform.

www.ingramcontent.com/pod-product-compliance
Lightning Source LLC
LaVergne TN
LVHW050556160826
845677LV00011B/2337